BUILDING GREAT TEAMS

Based on *Workshop Culture* by Alison Coward

First published in Great Britain by Practical Inspiration Publishing, 2025

© Alison Coward and Practical Inspiration Publishing, 2025

The moral rights of the author have been asserted.

ISBN   978-1-78860-744-5 (paperback)
           978-1-78860-745-2 (epub)
           978-1-78860-746-9 (Kindle)

All rights reserved. This book, or any portion thereof, may not be reproduced without the express written permission of the publisher.

Every effort has been made to trace copyright holders and to obtain their permission for the use of copyright material. The publisher apologizes for any errors or omissions and would be grateful if notified of any corrections that should be incorporated in future reprints or editions of this book.

EU GPSR representative: LOGOS EUROPE, 9 rue Nicolas Poussin, LA ROCHELLE 17000, France Contact@logoseurope.eu

Want to bulk-buy copies of this book for your team and colleagues? We can customize the content and co-brand *Building Great Teams* to suit your business's needs.

Please email info@practicalinspiration.com for more details.

Contents

Series introduction iv
Introduction 1
Day 1: The myth of teamwork 7
Day 2: A blueprint for great teams 16
Day 3: Less meeting, more momentum 27
Day 4: Mastering soft skills 37
Day 5: Alignment: seeing the bigger picture 48
Day 6: Cohesion: self-awareness and connection 58
Day 7: Communication: meetings and workshops ... 68
Day 8: Design: designing ways of working 77
Day 9: Change: continuous improvement 88
Day 10: Great teams that last 98
Conclusion 107
Endnotes 112

Series introduction

Welcome to *6-Minute Smarts*!

This is a series of very short books with one simple purpose: to introduce you to ideas that can make life and work better, and to give you time and space to think about how those ideas might apply to your life and work.

Each book introduces you to ten powerful ideas, but ideas on their own are useless – that's why each idea is followed by self-coaching questions to help you work out the 'so what?' for you in just six minutes of exploratory writing. What's exploratory writing? It's the kind of writing you do just for yourself, fast and free, without worrying what anyone else thinks. It's not just about getting ideas out of your head and onto paper where you can see them, it's about finding new connections and insights as you write. This is where the magic happens.

Find out more...

Introduction

What would it feel like to go to work every day, thrive alongside your colleagues and perform at your absolute best? Imagine a workplace where collaboration is nourishing, creativity flourishes and every individual's unique contributions are valued. This is the essence of great teamwork – a dynamic where alignment exists alongside individuality and progress feels both purposeful and energizing.

You may have experienced a glimpse of this during a particularly productive, well-facilitated workshop. These sessions bring teams together with clarity, creativity and focus, offering a sense of momentum that can feel almost magical. But when the workshop ends, and teams return to their daily routines, that magic often fades. This book explores how to capture and sustain that energy in everyday work by introducing a workshop culture.

Who is it for? Anyone who wants to create healthier, more effective teams. Whether you're a leader aiming to improve team dynamics, a team member looking to work better with others or an HR professional driving cultural change, you'll find practical guidance here.

The importance of teams in a fast-changing world

Teamwork has always been essential, but today it's more critical – and complex – than ever. The workplace has evolved into a fast-paced environment where collaboration isn't just an advantage but a necessity. The knowledge economy demands constant problem-solving, innovation and adaptability. Organizations that want to stay competitive must not only bring in top talent but also enable that talent to collaborate effectively.

Yet, despite the widespread focus on teamwork, many teams still fall short. Miscommunication, personality clashes and unclear goals are common barriers, compounded by heavy workloads, tighter deadlines and limited resources. These challenges can make maintaining momentum from the idea generation phase through to project completion seem impossible. Research backs this up: a *Harvard Business*

Review article reports that 75% of cross-functional teams are dysfunctional.[1] Clearly, the need for better teamwork has never been greater.

A framework for success

The concept of *workshop culture* offers a way forward. It's a team culture inspired by the principles and practices of workshops, designed to foster creativity, productivity and effective collaboration. In this culture, teams intentionally design how they work together, paying attention to how they communicate, align and solve problems.

Unlike traditional team-building approaches, workshop culture focuses on integrating collaborative practices into daily work. It's not a one-size-fits-all model – it's tailored to each team, putting people at the centre and valuing everyone's expertise. Teams that adopt a workshop culture have open communication, meaningful meetings and a clear sense of purpose.

Workshop culture also embraces healthy conflict and ambiguity. It's not about creating a frictionless environment but about using facilitation techniques to navigate complexity and find clarity together. This approach is equally effective for in-office, remote and hybrid teams.

By embedding the collaborative principles of workshops into everyday workflows, teams can achieve lasting change. This isn't just about running better workshops – it's about transforming how teams work together overall.

The five pillars of workshop culture

This book introduces a five-pillar framework to guide teams in building a workshop culture. Each pillar represents a critical element of high-performing teams:

1. **Alignment:** defining a shared vision and values to ensure the team moves in the same direction
2. **Cohesion:** developing empathy and understanding to strengthen connections and leverage individual strengths
3. **Communication:** running more effective, interactive meetings that foster meaningful discussions and decision-making
4. **Design:** creating intentional ways of working, from routines and rituals to workflows and collaboration methods
5. **Change:** embedding new habits and behaviours to sustain a workshop culture over time

Introduction

Chapters 5–9 cover these pillars in detail, providing practical tools to help you help your team build these capabilities step by step.

Why workshop culture matters

The principles of workshop culture align closely with the demands of today's workplace. They reflect the kind of leadership modern organizations need: empowering people to contribute their best, fostering an environment where ideas thrive and building trust through facilitation and shared ownership.

When teams consistently operate with the intentionality of a workshop culture, the results are transformative. They communicate more openly, experiment with new ideas and support each other in achieving shared goals. Work becomes less about navigating obstacles and more about uncovering possibilities.

The benefits also extend beyond the team. High-performing teams influence the wider organization, inspiring other teams to adopt similar practices. Workshop culture can start small – with one team – but its ripple effects can change an entire organization.

Building great teams isn't about sweeping changes or quick fixes – it's about cultivating habits, designing intentional workflows, and fostering an environment where collaboration thrives. By adopting a workshop culture, you can transform the way your team works and unlock its full potential.

You're ready to start. Over the next ten chapters (ten days, if you fancy treating this as a mini-course), you're going to discover ten key principles of listening as a leader and experiment with using them for yourself.

Let's go!

Day 1
The myth of teamwork

Collaboration is essential in modern organizations, yet it's often misunderstood and difficult to implement effectively. As a result, poor collaboration has a tangible impact on our work experience, performance and organizational culture.

In this chapter, we'll explore what stops us from collaborating effectively, the consequences of ineffective meetings and the critical relationship between engagement and performance at work.

The challenge of true collaboration

Modern organizations rely on effective teamwork, but collaboration often falls short. A 2019 Deloitte study found that shifting to team-based structures significantly improves performance,[2] yet collaboration doesn't come naturally – it requires effort and systemic support.

On an individual level, it's tempting to work alone for speed and simplicity, avoiding perspectives that might challenge our ideas. As the old saying goes, 'If you want to go fast, go alone; if you want to go far, go together.'

In teams, differences in personalities, work styles and priorities can cause friction, especially when there's no clear, collective goal to guide the group. Without a long-term perspective, it's hard to persist through the challenges of teamwork, particularly amid pressing deadlines.

At the organizational level, many systems and processes fail to support collaboration. For instance, when individuals are rewarded primarily for individual achievements, collaboration takes a back seat to competition. While collaboration is the rational choice for leveraging expertise, it becomes harder to prioritize when it isn't built into formal systems of recognition or compensation.

Despite these challenges, organizations that fail to foster true collaboration face three significant impacts: bad meetings, low engagement and a lack of purpose.

Impact 1: bad meetings

Meetings are a cornerstone of teamwork, but poorly run meetings waste time and money. In the US, employees spend an average of 6 hours a week in meetings, with senior managers attending up to 23 hours. A 2019 study by Doodle estimated that poorly organized meetings cost over $450 billion across the US and the UK.[3]

However, the issue isn't the meetings themselves – it's how they're run. Meetings can be valuable opportunities for collaboration, but too often they feel like distractions from real work.

Research shows that bad meetings not only harm productivity but also impact team performance and organizational success. Positive meetings – those that include constructive interactions like problem-solving and action planning – boost team performance for years. In contrast, meetings filled with negativity, such as complaints or criticism, have long-lasting detrimental effects.[4]

Meetings also shape how employees feel about their work. Positive, energizing meetings leave teams feeling valued, motivated and ready to take action. On the other hand, meetings that drain energy or add unnecessary workload lead to frustration and disengagement.

Making meetings better doesn't require radical changes. Simple steps, such as starting and ending on time, ensuring relevance and fostering open communication, can transform meetings into productive and engaging spaces.[5]

Ultimately, meetings are a reflection of an organization's culture. Poorly run meetings signal deeper issues, while well-designed ones can set the tone for effective collaboration.

Impact 2: low engagement

Employee engagement is critical to performance, yet most organizations struggle to foster it. A 2017 Gallup report famously revealed that 85% of employees were not engaged or were actively disengaged at work.[6] This lack of engagement directly affects productivity and organizational success.

High engagement correlates with high performance. Research has shown that teams with above-average engagement are 70% more successful than those with below-average engagement.[7] Leaders who prioritize creating supportive, engaging workplaces reap the benefits of higher productivity and employee satisfaction.

There's a misconception that high performance and employee well-being are at odds, but the two are deeply interconnected. A happy, engaged culture supports high performance, and vice versa. When employees feel empowered to do meaningful work without unnecessary barriers, they are more engaged and productive.

As Teresa Amabile and Steven Kramer demonstrate in *The Progress Principle*, enabling progress and removing obstacles are the most important factors in creating a positive and engaged workplace.[8] By focusing on these fundamentals, organizations can create environments where employees thrive.

Impact 3: lack of purpose

Purpose is becoming a non-negotiable element of work. In 2018, BetterUp reported that nine out of ten people would take a pay cut for more meaningful work.[9] Given that employees spend about a third of their lives at work, it's no surprise they want to feel fulfilled by what they do.

A lack of purpose in the workplace has serious consequences for employee retention. The 'Great Resignation' of 2021 highlighted this, as millions of people left unfulfilling jobs in search of something more meaningful. Employers that fail to address the growing demand for purpose risk losing talent and weakening their organizations.

Creating purpose doesn't require grand gestures. It's about giving employees opportunities to grow, learn and make a difference. When people feel their work matters, they are more likely to stay engaged and committed to their organization.

Creating a culture of collaboration

Overcoming the challenges of teamwork requires intentional effort. Organizations need to move beyond passive approaches to collaboration and actively design their working practices. One way to do this is by fostering a workshop culture.

Workshops offer structured opportunities for teams to collaborate, share ideas and solve problems. Whether your team is thriving or struggling, a workshop culture can help.

- For high-performing teams, workshops act as a preventative measure, maintaining team health and momentum.
- For teams facing challenges, workshops serve as a remedy, addressing issues and reigniting engagement.

The myth of teamwork

Workshops also help embed collaboration into an organization's culture. When meetings and team interactions are intentionally designed, they set the stage for better teamwork and improved outcomes.

By prioritizing collaboration and addressing the barriers that hinder it, organizations can move beyond the myth of teamwork and create cultures where true collaboration thrives.

 So what? Over to you...

1. Does the way your meetings work right now help or hinder collaboration? How could you make them better?

2. What supports engagement in your team... and what hinders it?

3. How can you find opportunities this week to allow team members to connect with purpose – e.g. by connecting their work to the bigger picture?

Day 2
A blueprint for great teams

In this chapter, we'll explore how workshops can address the challenges of teamwork by fostering equal contributions, open communication and curiosity. Workshops provide a practical solution to help teams collaborate effectively, and we'll unpack the elements that make them successful. We'll also examine the essential components of high-performing team cultures.

Case study: discovering workshop culture

I didn't always realize the transformative power of workshops. Early in my career, I worked as a facilitator, helping teams address specific challenges in short, one-off sessions. My involvement ended

A blueprint for great teams

once the workshop was over – until a client requested my help in formalizing their company values.

We began with a small group of executives, including the CEO. Using sticky notes, we captured words and phrases that defined the company, identified themes and voted on the most representative values. Later, the client invited me to replicate the process with their entire senior leadership team during a strategy meeting.

When I entered the room, I faced a long conference table at which over 20 people were seated. Their standard meeting format – business updates, lunch and casual discussion – wasn't conducive to focused collaboration. The CEO chaired the meeting and dominated the agenda, and they rarely finished all their planned discussions. Few participants spoke, and the length of the table itself was intimidating.

I introduced a new format, distributing sticky notes and markers and dividing the group into smaller teams for discussions. The energy in the room changed as everyone actively participated. By the end of the session, the broader group had reaffirmed the original values, demonstrating alignment and a strong sense of identity.

The workshop didn't just produce outcomes – it changed how the team worked together. Over time, they adopted new meeting formats, including dedicated sessions for innovation and problem-solving. Connections between team members strengthened, and the culture began to shift. That's when I realized a workshop isn't just about what happens in the room – it has the power to transform team culture.

Why workshops foster great team culture

Workshops exemplify the characteristics of high-performing teams, creating environments where collaboration thrives. Let's explore the key characteristics of a workshop so that we can see how it is relevant to a team culture.

True collaboration

Workshops provide the structure and practice teams need to collaborate effectively. With clear facilitation, teams can bring together diverse perspectives and talents to solve complex problems.

True collaboration ensures that everyone's ideas contribute to the final outcome, even if individual contributions become indistinguishable in the final product. In this process, participants celebrate collective achievements rather than seeking individual recognition.

Facilitation

A great facilitator, by subtly guiding the process, creates an environment where teams focus on outcomes. Unlike a meeting chair, who controls the agenda, a facilitator encourages participation and keeps discussions on track without dominating the conversation.

Facilitators don't need to be subject matter experts. Their role is to create a space where the team can problem-solve together, fostering autonomy and engagement. Leaders who adopt this approach empower their teams to take ownership of their work while maintaining alignment and focus.

Equal contributions and engagement

Workshops level the playing field, ensuring everyone's voice is heard, regardless of seniority, background or role. By breaking down hierarchical dynamics, workshops tap into the full potential of the team.

This inclusive approach promotes innovation and creativity while fostering a sense of belonging.

Employees feel valued when their contributions are acknowledged, leading to greater engagement and stronger team connections.

Open communication and visible progress

Workshops often involve tools like sticky notes, whiteboards or digital platforms to capture ideas in real time. These creations make abstract concepts tangible, helping teams connect ideas, track progress and visualize outcomes.

Visible progress keeps the team motivated, fosters transparency and ensures everyone stays aligned. Teams can also identify and address potential conflicts or bottlenecks early, ensuring smoother workflows.

Curiosity, learning and experimentation

Workshops encourage teams to explore new ideas, challenge assumptions and embrace experimentation. In this low-pressure environment, participants feel free to share unfinished thoughts and make mistakes, knowing they are part of a collective learning process.

Curiosity is a catalyst for innovation and high performance. By fostering a mindset of exploration, workshops help teams develop new insights and creative solutions.

A blueprint for great teams

Responsiveness and adaptability

Even the most carefully planned workshops require flexibility to meet the group's evolving needs. Facilitators adapt to emerging priorities, demonstrating how teams can navigate ambiguity and unexpected challenges.

This responsiveness builds resilience, helping teams stay grounded and make progress even when circumstances change. The ability to adapt is a critical skill for modern organizations facing rapid change and uncertainty.

Tolerance for ambiguity

Workshops teach teams to embrace the creative messiness of problem-solving. Ideas are rarely linear, and the process often involves trial and error. This mindset encourages teams to take risks, explore unconventional approaches and innovate.

While workshops may appear unstructured to an outsider, they often follow a carefully crafted process that maximizes creativity and productivity. By embracing this approach, teams can achieve better outcomes and apply these principles to their daily work.

What you are designing for in a workshop culture

To start considering how your team will work together as a result of a workshop culture, you first need to get clear on the environment you are designing. What makes a great team culture? These are the same elements that make workshops great.

Psychological safety

Psychological safety is the foundation of high-performing teams. It allows members to speak up, share ideas and take risks without fear of judgment or negative consequences. Research by Google's Project Aristotle found that psychological safety is the most important factor in team success, outweighing individual talent.[10]

Workshops create spaces where psychological safety thrives. By embedding this principle into daily team interactions, organizations can unlock trust and creativity and get better results.

Diversity

Diverse teams bring together a range of perspectives and experiences, leading to richer discussions and more innovative solutions. However, diversity alone isn't enough – it must be accompanied by an inclusive environment where all voices are heard.

Workshops celebrate differences and help teams navigate the tension that can arise from opposing viewpoints. By valuing diverse perspectives, teams can achieve better outcomes while fostering mutual respect and understanding.

Healthy conflict

Conflict is a natural part of collaboration, but it must be managed constructively. Workshops provide a safe space for productive conflict, where ideas can be challenged without personal tensions. This openness to conflict leads to better decisions and more creative solutions.

Autonomy and transparency

Workshops show teams how to take ownership of their work while staying aligned with shared goals. Transparency – whether through visible artifacts or open communication – keeps everyone informed and ensures accountability without micromanagement.

When teams feel autonomous and connected, they are more productive and engaged, creating a positive cycle of performance and satisfaction.

Conclusion

Workshops are more than just one-off events – they are powerful tools for building great teams. By embedding the principles of workshops into team culture, organizations can overcome the challenges of collaboration and unlock their teams' full potential.

Convinced? Then let's dive into the four foundations of workshop culture.

 So what? Over to you...

1. Which of the workshop characteristics is most useful for your team right now? Why?

A blueprint for great teams

2. Which of the elements of great team culture is most challenging for your team right now? Why?

3. In light of your answers above, what action might you take this week?

Day 3
Less meeting, more momentum

A *workshop culture* isn't just about occasional workshops; it's a team culture that applies the principles of workshops – creativity, facilitation and collaboration – in daily work. By making these practices part of team dynamics, organizations can foster ingenuity, productivity and connection.

In this chapter, we'll explore the four foundations of a workshop culture: seeing workshops as more than one-off events; balancing creativity and productivity; focusing on small, iterative changes; and designing team dynamics for success.

Foundation 1: workshops are more than a one-off event

Workshops are distinct from routine work. They involve focused, dedicated time where teams collaborate, ideate and problem-solve in a different way. Whether conducted in person or online, workshops create a space that signals *this is not business as usual*.

- **The time:** Workshops stand out because they require teams to step away from the daily grind and engage fully. These sessions are planned, structured and purposeful – helping teams explore ideas or solve challenges they might otherwise ignore.
- **The space and setup:** Physical workshop spaces feel different. Creative set-ups, like sticky notes, flip charts or quirky environments, encourage experimentation and creativity. Virtual workshops replicate this with online tools like whiteboards, signalling a shift in how teams think and work.
- **The people and relationships:** Workshops create environments where participants feel free to open up, connect and share ideas more deeply than in regular meetings. With the

right facilitation, teams develop trust, enjoy their work and collaborate more effectively.

In a workshop culture, these practices become embedded in daily work. Collaboration and open communication stop being one-off experiences and become how teams naturally operate.

Foundation 2: balance creativity and productivity

Workshops are often associated with creativity and ideation, which can seem at odds with task-focused productivity. Organizations tend to prioritize execution over exploration because creativity feels inefficient and unpredictable. However, creativity and productivity are not opposites – they are interconnected.

When balanced effectively, creativity generates innovative ideas, while productivity turns those ideas into actionable outcomes. A workshop culture encourages this balance by embracing creativity as part of everyday work, not something confined to occasional brainstorming sessions.

- **Creating space for creativity:** Leaders must understand and facilitate creativity to make it effective. It requires flexibility and freedom, guided by clear parameters such as deadlines, briefs or budgets. While the process might appear chaotic, trust in its value leads to stronger execution. Workshops illustrate this balance perfectly. They move between divergent thinking (exploration and idea generation) and convergent thinking (narrowing focus and making decisions). This rhythm helps teams create tangible outcomes from abstract ideas.

- **Leading through uncertainty:** Creative processes can feel uncomfortable, especially when progress isn't immediate. Workshops teach teams to navigate this ambiguity, guided by facilitators who reassure participants and help them find clarity. In a workshop culture, this tolerance for uncertainty becomes a key strength, enabling teams to stay creative and productive.

Foundation 3: make tiny tweaks, not sweeping changes

Transitioning to a workshop culture doesn't happen overnight. Instead of sweeping reforms, small, incremental changes are the key to sustainable transformation.

Start small, build momentum

A single, well-run workshop can introduce teams to a new way of working, often contrasting sharply with unproductive meetings. Over time, regular workshops can reinforce these practices, gradually integrating workshop principles into everyday work. Here's what the journey towards a fully fledged workshop culture might look like for your team:

1. **One-off workshops:** Teams experience the benefits of a structured, collaborative session, often achieving more in a few hours than they might in weeks of standard meetings.
2. **Regular workshops:** As workshops become more frequent, teams begin to incorporate workshop techniques – like brainstorming or visualizing ideas – into their regular meetings.
3. **Workshop culture:** Eventually, workshop practices and mindsets permeate the team's daily interactions, transforming how they work together.

This transition is iterative and non-linear, with small shifts leading to big impacts. Teams recognize the value of improved meetings and naturally adopt better collaboration habits.

Foundation 4: a workshop culture is intentionally designed

A workshop culture doesn't happen by accident. Like a great workshop, it must be intentionally designed to foster collaboration, connection and progress.

- **Designing for group dynamics:** Every team has dynamics that can either hinder or enhance collaboration. For example, dominant voices may overshadow quieter team members, or groupthink may stifle diverse ideas. Facilitators address these challenges by designing activities that encourage equal participation and bring out all perspectives. Teams adopting a workshop culture can apply the same principles to their daily work – breaking into smaller groups for discussions, encouraging reflection or using tools to capture everyone's input. These practices create environments where creativity and collaboration thrive.
- **Designing for progress:** Workshops are structured to help teams move forward. A facilitator crafts a clear narrative, anticipating roadblocks and creating activities to overcome them. In a workshop culture, teams approach

challenges with the same mindset: identifying barriers, designing solutions and celebrating progress.
- **Designing for connection:** In a task-driven world, human connection is often overlooked. Workshops remind us of the importance of slowing down, relating to one another and building trust. This connection isn't just a nice-to-have – it's a critical factor in team performance. Research from the MIT Human Dynamics Lab shows that teams with frequent, informal communication perform better.[11] By integrating opportunities for connection into daily work, teams build stronger relationships and improve collaboration.

Conclusion

These four foundations of a workshop culture offer a blueprint for building momentum and achieving success. By adopting these principles, teams can transform their culture, making collaboration, innovation and connection part of their everyday work. But how can you make that happen? Read on...

So what? Over to you…

1. Which of these principles is strongest in your team right now? How can you build on that?

2. Which of these principles is weakest in your team right now? How might you address that?

3. Think about the meetings in your diary this week. Where is there an opportunity to bring in an idea from this chapter?

Day 4
Mastering soft skills

Building a workshop culture will require some shifts in your thinking, mindset and behaviour. As the one initiating the change, you'll need some essential core skills. This chapter prepares you for the practical implementation that will come next.

The challenge of change

One of my clients, Louise (name changed), learned first-hand how challenging it can be to change behaviours within a team. A respected leader with extensive experience in creative technology, Louise inherited a team that was burned out, unhappy and stressed. Her vision was to create a thriving, collaborative and supportive workplace – a stark contrast to the culture her team had known.

Building Great Teams

While Louise was passionate about improving her team's work environment, she underestimated how hard it would be to bring everyone on the journey.

First, we had to understand that nothing would happen overnight and we would only see the change looking back over a period of time. We couldn't expect to see this daily, or even weekly. It might even take a few months for some changes to really take hold.

Then we had to accept what was in our control and what wasn't. Some people had more work to do to build emotional intelligence, and we had to explore how to work with this, at their speed, rather than constantly knocking at a door that wasn't ready to open.

This meant continuing the momentum with those who were positive about change, while working directly and sensitively with those who may have been unintentionally (or intentionally!) blocking progress.

We also had to be prepared for what I call the 'point of no return'. This stage feels like clearing out a long-neglected cupboard: initially, pulling everything out creates a bigger mess, making it seem like things are worse. But once you're in the thick of it, turning back isn't an option and persistence is the only way forward.

Over six months, Louise demonstrated relentless commitment. She attended every workshop alongside her team, reinforcing the importance of their collective learning. Conversations about workshop outcomes became regular topics in team meetings, ensuring the changes became part of their broader business planning.

Small wins were crucial. Each week, I encouraged Louise to note shifts in behaviour, fresh ideas or new energy in meetings. These incremental changes added up to significant progress. By the end of our engagement, her team had not only embraced facilitation principles in their planning but also developed a roadmap to sustain the transformation.

The role of a change agent

Building a workshop culture means stepping into the role of a change agent, and that requires a shift in how you approach change.

Most of us are used to changes with a clear start, middle and end – like moving to a new home or starting a job. But creating a workshop culture is different. There's no finish line; it's a continuous process. New projects, opportunities and external influences will always require adjustments.

This ongoing evolution requires a mindset shift – for you and your team. It's about fundamentally altering how you think and work together.

What you can control

As a change agent, it's essential to recognize what's within your control and what isn't. You'll encounter resistance – whether from deep-rooted habits, fear of the unknown or systems that are slow to shift. Tackling everything at once is overwhelming, so start with small, achievable wins.

Map out your vision and long-term goals, then identify where you have the most influence. Stephen Covey's *7 Habits of Highly Effective People* introduces the concept of three circles: your circle of control (what you can directly impact), your circle of influence (what you can shape indirectly) and your circle of concern (factors beyond your reach).[12] Focus on what you can control, and take small steps to create momentum.

Celebrate small wins along the way, even if immediate progress feels invisible. Over time, these incremental shifts will add up and you'll see how far you've come.

Mastering collaboration

At the heart of a workshop culture is collaboration. This starts with believing in the value of others' insights and being genuinely curious about their perspectives. True collaboration requires letting go of control and trusting your team to contribute meaningfully.

For leaders accustomed to having all the answers, this can be a challenging transition. It means admitting when you don't know something, asking open-ended questions and embracing the uncertainty that comes with hearing diverse viewpoints. While this may feel uncomfortable at first, it creates the foundation for stronger, more connected teams.

The hard work of soft skills

Building a workshop culture demands more than technical expertise – it requires mastering interpersonal skills and emotional intelligence. Here are some key soft skills that are vital for success:

- **Letting go of control:** Shift from trying to predict and control outcomes to setting the foundation for your team to achieve the best results themselves.
- **Trust:** Have confidence in your team's ability and show that you trust them. This fosters ownership and investment in their work.
- **Handling uncertainty:** Accept that you won't have all the answers immediately. Problem-

solving is an ongoing process, and sitting with uncertainty is essential for collaboration.
- **Openness:** Be genuinely curious about others' ideas, even if they challenge your own. Collaboration is about inviting input and being willing to adjust based on others' contributions.
- **Vulnerability:** Experimentation and innovation come with risks and mistakes. Owning your missteps sets the tone for authentic, open conversations within your team.

Facilitation: the key to collaboration

Facilitation lies at the core of a workshop culture. While managers often direct tasks, facilitators guide processes, creating space for others to collaborate effectively. Facilitators focus on inclusion, participation and engagement, ensuring every voice is heard and every perspective valued.

In a workshop culture, facilitation serves two purposes:

1. **Content-focused facilitation:** Workshops generate ideas, solutions and plans that drive business outcomes.

2. **Process-focused facilitation:** Workshops help teams reflect on how they work together, fostering stronger collaboration and communication.

Facilitation principles eventually permeate all aspects of a team's interactions, from meetings to everyday conversations. This shift fosters a collaborative environment that sustains itself over time.

Introducing a workshop culture involves leading your team through both the creative process and the behaviour changes necessary for lasting impact. Generating ideas is just the beginning; translating those ideas into action requires motivation, empathy, and persistence.

Building for the long term

Behaviour change doesn't happen overnight. Even with the best intentions, adopting new habits and overcoming resistance takes time. Facilitators and leaders alike must create exercises and follow-ups that nudge teams toward sustainable change.

The process of building a workshop culture mirrors the process of running a workshop. It involves three stages:

1. **Preparation:** Understand your goals and design a clear path forward.
2. **Guidance:** Use facilitation skills to encourage inclusivity and collaboration.
3. **Embedding:** Translate ideas into actionable changes, ensuring new behaviours become part of daily work.

Unlike a workshop, however, a workshop culture has no defined endpoint. It's an ongoing journey of learning, adapting and evolving together.

Conclusion

Mastering soft skills like collaboration and facilitation is central to building a workshop culture. These skills, together with emotional intelligence, will help you guide your team through change, foster deeper connections and create an environment where creativity and productivity thrive.

By focusing on small, achievable steps and embracing the challenges of change, you can build a culture that evolves continuously, enabling your team to meet new challenges with confidence and resilience.

In the next five chapters I'll take you through a framework for building a workshop culture. The framework is made up of five pillars:

1. **Alignment:** seeing the bigger picture
2. **Cohesion:** building self-awareness and empathy
3. **Communication:** meetings and workshops
4. **Design:** building new ways of working
5. **Change:** shifting behaviour and habits

While the pillars are set out in this order, you may find that there is a particular area that you want to address first based on the health of your team. Start wherever feels right to you.

So what? Over to you...

1. What does it mean to think of yourself as a change agent? What's exciting/worrying about that?

2. Which of the soft skills listed in this chapter will you aim to work on this week, and how?

Mastering soft skills

3. How might you facilitate rather than manage an interaction this week?

Day 5
Alignment: seeing the bigger picture

The first step in building a workshop culture is to align your team around the bigger picture. This means ensuring everyone is oriented in the same direction before any work begins. Misalignment, if not addressed early, can derail progress and hinder potential. Alignment is about shared purpose, clarity and commitment, and this sets the stage for your team's transformation.

Case study: speeding up through alignment

Alignment can feel like a tug of war. When team members pull in different directions, progress stalls. I

Alignment: seeing the bigger picture

saw this first-hand with a talented team struggling to agree on the direction for their venture.

When the team first formed, they shared similar aspirations. Over time, their personal goals evolved and they began to see the business differently. This led to tension, a breakdown in relationships and stagnation. Despite their initial closeness, they couldn't understand why they were no longer aligned.

To address this, I worked with each person individually to clarify their core values, then facilitated group discussions to assess alignment. It became clear that some individual values were too different for the team to move forward together. They made the difficult decision to part ways.

The process, though painful, accelerated progress for everyone. Those with aligned visions stayed and grew the business, while others pursued fulfilling new paths. By identifying misalignment, we avoided further stress and enabled all parties to move forward.

Sometimes, building a workshop culture uncovers fundamental misalignments. While difficult, addressing these gaps ultimately leads to better outcomes for individuals and the team. ~

Dynamic and fluid teams

Today's challenges evolve rapidly, requiring teams to adapt quickly. Most people belong to multiple teams simultaneously, each with its own dynamic and culture. This complexity demands flexibility and an ability to switch contexts seamlessly.

Team culture is shaped by three factors:

1. **Team members:** Each individual brings unique skills, experiences and perspectives.
2. **Work:** The nature of the team's responsibilities influences its pace, timelines and interactions.
3. **Context:** External factors, such as organizational changes or market conditions, impact how the team operates.

These elements create a team's unique culture, which evolves whenever the team's composition, work or context changes. Leaders must monitor and adapt to these shifts, fostering alignment despite fluidity.

The mindset of a dynamic team

To thrive in a workshop culture, teams must develop four essential mindsets:

Alignment: seeing the bigger picture

1. **Growth mindset:** the belief that collaboration can improve through practice and persistence
2. **Design mindset:** an intentional approach to teamwork, shaping how collaboration happens
3. **Facilitation mindset:** skills to guide inclusive, effective discussions and decision-making
4. **Change mindset:** the ability to adapt and embrace new ways of working

A growth mindset lays the foundation, encouraging teams to believe in their capacity for improvement. The design and facilitation mindsets provide tools for implementing collaborative practices, while the change mindset ensures the team can adapt behaviours and take action.

The value of a growth mindset

Carol Dweck's *Mindset* introduced the concept of a growth mindset – the commitment to improvement through effort and learning. In contrast, a fixed mindset assumes abilities are static and success should come effortlessly.[13]

In teams, we often romanticize the idea of natural chemistry, assuming high performance will emerge automatically when talented individuals come together. However, collaboration, like any skill, requires deliberate effort. Emotional intelligence, curiosity and patience are as crucial as technical expertise for team success.

High-performing teams actively work on their connections, understanding that great collaboration doesn't happen by chance.

Setting direction: alignment, clarity and purpose

Alignment is the launch pad for high performance, and collective clarity provides the fuel. A shared understanding of the team's purpose grounds them, enabling forward momentum despite uncertainty. When teams are clear on what matters, they can focus less on micromanagement and more on achieving shared goals.

Facilitated workshops are ideal for fostering alignment. They encourage teams to think broadly, explore possibilities and align on a shared vision. This process not only creates a sense of purpose but also energizes teams to collaborate effectively.

Purpose and motivation

A clear sense of purpose is essential for engagement at work. In *Drive*, Daniel Pink identifies purpose, along

Alignment: seeing the bigger picture

with autonomy and mastery, as key motivators.[14] Teams that understand how their contributions fit into a larger vision are more connected and motivated to overcome challenges.

Big-picture thinking strengthens this connection. By stepping back from day-to-day details, teams can identify patterns, generate new insights and empower themselves to shape their work.

Translating alignment into action

Workshops teach us that clarity on outcomes drives progress. Similarly, aligning your team's vision, values and goals creates the framework for success.

1. **Vision and values:** Define your team's purpose and the principles that guide your work. These act as a compass, keeping your team grounded during change and uncertainty.
2. **Strategy and goals:** Turn big-picture thinking into actionable steps. Prioritize ideas, allocate resources and create a timeline for progress.
3. **Accountability:** Establish systems to track progress and keep the team focused on shared objectives.

Team values, in particular, are a foundation for long-term alignment. They guide behaviour, decision-making and collaboration, ensuring consistency as the team evolves.

Designing and living your values

Good values act as a GPS, guiding decision-making and fostering a strong team identity. To make values meaningful, they must translate into specific behaviours. For example, a value like 'curiosity' might translate into regularly asking questions before proposing solutions.

To embed values in daily work, capture them visually, discuss them regularly in team meetings and celebrate examples of those values in action. Over time, these consistent practices reinforce alignment and strengthen the team's culture.

Conclusion

Alignment is the cornerstone of high-performing teams. By defining a shared vision, setting clear values and fostering a growth mindset, teams can align around a compelling purpose and sustain momentum. This clarity empowers teams to navigate change, work collaboratively and achieve their goals together.

Alignment: seeing the bigger picture

So what? Over to you…

1. How clear is your team on their collective goals? What could you do this week to check on alignment?

2. What are your team values? How can you be sure your team is living them in practice?

Alignment: seeing the bigger picture

3. How do you keep each other accountable? What method could you introduce this week?

Day 6
Cohesion: self-awareness and connection

Once a team aligns on its vision and values, each member must understand their role and contribution. This self-awareness fosters empathy and creates strong connections that make collaboration smoother. Cohesion enables teams to navigate challenges, such as giving feedback or resolving conflict, with greater ease.

Cohesion is about balancing individual identity with team identity. When team members develop self-awareness, they recognize their unique strengths while understanding how they fit into the larger group. This balance is crucial for high performance, encouraging productive collaboration rooted in trust and mutual respect.

Cohesion: self-awareness and connection

Case study: solving a personality clash

Even with shared goals, personality clashes can obstruct collaboration. I worked with a team delivering high-quality programmes where two individuals clashed due to opposing working styles.

One was high energy, results driven and willing to work long hours, while the other valued relationship-building and a balanced workweek. Their disagreements often escalated, causing tension for the rest of the team. Other members felt stuck in a power struggle, diverting time and energy away from productive work.

To resolve this, the team engaged in deep conversations about their working styles. Each member created a 'user manual', sharing insights such as:

- what kind of work and what kind of environments help them thrive
- how to get the best out of them
- situations where they might struggle

These discussions helped the two individuals understand their impact on the team. They committed to being more curious and patient with one another and began leveraging each other's strengths rather than forcing one approach. As a result, they moved past conflict and unlocked greater collaboration.

Balancing the team and the individual

For teams to perform at their best, individuals must thrive. Workshops often balance individual contributions with group dynamics, allowing participants to showcase their strengths while working toward a collective goal.

This principle applies to building cohesion. Effective teams celebrate diverse working styles and embrace the tensions they create, recognizing that innovation often stems from these differences.

Teams perform better when members understand their roles and responsibilities and how they contribute to the broader purpose. As self-awareness increases, so do qualities like emotional intelligence, empathy and collaboration – skills essential for high performance.

Building self-awareness for team performance

Starting with personality tests

Personality assessments like Myers-Briggs, Belbin, Enneagram, DISC and StrengthsFinder can provide a useful entry point for self-awareness. These tools help team members articulate their working styles and understand differences within the group. However, assessments are just a starting point. To maximize their value, teams should:

1. Reflect on the results and discuss them
2. Identify points of conflict or alignment
3. Explore how to collaborate more effectively

The reflection habit

True self-awareness requires regular reflection. By examining their reactions, working preferences and communication styles, individuals can better understand themselves and their impact on the team. This habit improves both individual and team performance.

Key areas for reflection include:

1. **Unique skills and expertise:** strengths and areas for growth
2. **Working preferences:** productivity patterns, tasks they enjoy or struggle with
3. **Collaboration skills:** communication and interaction with others

When reflection becomes a regular part of work, it helps teams align personal contributions with collective goals, fostering mutual growth and accountability.

Supporting individual and team productivity

Collaboration doesn't mean constantly working together. Research shows the best teamwork happens in bursts, punctuated by periods of focused individual work.[15] Balancing these modes is critical for both individual and team productivity.

A *workshop culture* encourages team members to share their working styles and routines, recognizing that productivity is deeply personal. For instance, some might excel in the morning, while others perform better later in the day. Acknowledging these differences improves overall effectiveness, especially in remote or global teams.

Encourage team members to develop personal productivity systems, experimenting with routines, tools and techniques to find what works best for them. These systems enhance individual performance while contributing to the team's success.

Empathy as the foundation of cohesion

Empathy – the ability to understand and share others' perspectives – is vital for cohesive teams. It creates an inclusive, compassionate environment where members feel valued and conflicts are less likely to escalate.

Cohesion: self-awareness and connection

By fostering empathy, teams can better navigate tensions and celebrate diverse working styles. Tools like the 'empathy map canvas' created by Dave Gray[16] help teams understand what their customers might feel, think, say or do so that they can build better products and services. It's also a great tool to use within and across teams to build better understanding of different working styles, motivations and interpretations.

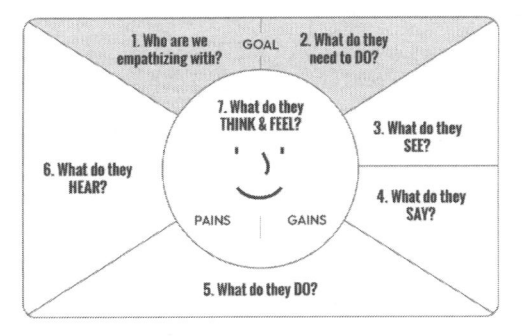

Figure 1 The empathy map canvas by Dave Gray. Redrawn by Gabija Jankauskaite; reproduced with permission.

Celebrating diversity and building trust

Great teams don't just tolerate differences – they celebrate them. Diversity in working styles and perspectives can lead to creative breakthroughs, but this also requires resilience and adaptability. Empathy helps teams embrace this diversity, turning potential conflicts into opportunities for growth.

When teams prioritize self-awareness, empathy and open communication, they create the conditions for true collaboration. This not only enhances performance but also builds a culture of trust, inclusion and continuous improvement.

Conclusion

Cohesion is the glue that binds aligned teams together. By fostering self-awareness, celebrating diversity and building empathy, teams can create strong connections that support productive collaboration. This foundation enables teams to navigate challenges, innovate and perform at their best.

Cohesion: self-awareness and connection

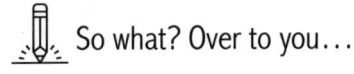

So what? Over to you...

1. What tool or practice might you use to build self-awareness within your team?

2. How might you help yourself and your team members develop personal productivity systems?

Cohesion: self-awareness and connection

3. How might you encourage empathy within your team?

Day 7
Communication: meetings and workshops

Communication sits at the heart of a high-performing team, and meetings are a critical mechanism for fostering collaboration and connection. This chapter explores how teams can reimagine meetings to become impactful, engaging and central to building a workshop culture. By embedding facilitation skills across the team and designing purposeful meeting rhythms, communication becomes a driver for productivity and team cohesion.

The role of meetings in team culture

Meetings are the linchpin of modern organizations. They are more than just opportunities to share

Communication: meetings and workshops

updates; they are the spaces where relationships are developed, ideas are born and team culture is built. Yet, as we've already seen, poorly run meetings can become an obstacle to collaboration. Without a clear purpose, they often descend into unproductive discussions dominated by opinions, egos and politics.

In a workshop culture, meetings take on a new form. They are intentionally designed to align with their purpose – whether that's brainstorming, decision-making or strategic planning – and are facilitated to ensure participation and progress. This shift transforms meetings from a dreaded necessity into a cornerstone of team success.

The case for facilitated meetings

Facilitated meetings provide structure and inclusivity, creating a space where all voices can contribute. Effective facilitation also strengthens team dynamics by improving communication, fostering empathy and encouraging accountability.

When everyone in a team understands facilitation skills, it creates a culture where collaboration thrives. Rotating the role of facilitator gives team members a chance to practise leadership and fosters shared responsibility for the team's success. This empowers individuals to raise concerns, suggest improvements and ensure meetings remain productive.

Practical steps to improve meetings

1. Design meetings with a clear purpose

Every meeting should begin with a well-defined purpose and desired outcomes. Start by asking:

- Why are we holding this meeting?
- What outputs do we need (e.g. a list of action points, a strategic plan, feedback on an idea)?
- What questions should guide the discussion?

These questions ensure that meetings are not only relevant but also focused on achieving specific goals.

2. Embrace the facilitation mindset

Facilitation begins with designing a meeting that encourages participation and ownership. Here's how:

- Create a safe, inclusive environment by inviting everyone to share their thoughts.
- Use check-ins or reflection questions at the start to set the tone and engage participants.

- Manage group dynamics by keeping the conversation focused, acknowledging all contributions and redirecting when necessary.

Facilitators should balance structure with flexibility, knowing when to adapt based on the group's energy and needs.

3. Encourage individual thinking and breakout discussions

Not all collaboration happens in large groups. Allocating time for individual reflection or small breakout groups within meetings allows participants to process ideas and contribute more meaningfully. This approach also supports diverse working styles, including those of introverted or neurodivergent team members.

4. Use visual tools to capture discussions

Visual elements, such as sticky notes, whiteboards or graphic facilitation, can help teams organize and clarify their ideas. These tools make abstract discussions tangible, promote inclusivity and create a record of the meeting that participants can refer back to.

Building a meeting rhythm

A strong meeting rhythm helps teams maintain momentum and accountability. This involves creating a calendar of regular meetings with clear purposes and frequencies. For example:

- **Weekly:** quick updates to address immediate challenges
- **Monthly:** deeper dives into strategic goals or team progress
- **Quarterly or annually:** reflection and planning for the bigger picture

Each meeting type should have a distinct structure, duration and focus. This rhythm becomes the heartbeat of the team, connecting daily tasks to long-term goals.

It's important to review and adjust meeting rhythms periodically. If certain meetings lose their value or a new need arises, adapt the schedule to ensure it continues to serve the team's needs.

Introducing 'workshop culture' sessions

In addition to task-oriented meetings, workshop culture involves a unique type of meeting focused

Communication: meetings and workshops

on *how* the team works together. These sessions are dedicated to reflecting on team dynamics, habits and processes.

Though they may seem like a distraction from daily work, these sessions are essential for fostering transparency, addressing blockers and co-creating better ways of working. Over time, they become a natural and integral part of team collaboration.

Maintaining momentum after meetings

The impact of a well-facilitated meeting extends beyond the session itself. To ensure follow-through:

- end each meeting with clear next steps, assigning specific actions to participants
- build accountability by revisiting these actions in subsequent meetings

This process bridges the gap between ideas and implementation, ensuring that discussions lead to meaningful progress.

The bigger picture of communication

Effective communication is about more than just meetings – it's about how a team connects, collaborates and creates together. Meetings are the visible part of this culture, but what happens between them – through day-to-day interactions, shared tools and ongoing reflection – is just as important.

By rethinking how meetings are designed and run, teams can build a communication culture that fosters connection, creativity and high performance. This creates a ripple effect, improving not only how teams work together but also the outcomes they achieve.

So what? Over to you...

1. Look back at those practical steps to improve meetings. Which could you try this week?

Communication: meetings and workshops

2. Think about the rhythm of your team's meetings. How could it work better?

3. What one thing could you do to maintain momentum after a significant meeting?

Day 8
Design: designing ways of working

Design is the process of intentionally crafting how a team works together to reach its highest potential. Once a team has aligned on its vision and values and built cohesion through self-awareness, it's time to focus on how to work better together. Design encourages teams to move beyond default practices, intentionally shaping routines, processes and tools to fit their unique culture and goals. This chapter explores how teams can build rituals, optimize productivity and integrate asynchronous work to overcome common challenges and create a thriving team environment.

Working by design, not by default

Many teams fall into reactive patterns of work, doing things the way they've always been done without questioning their effectiveness. This 'default' mode often leads to inefficiencies, frustration and burn-out.

In one example, a team of young professionals working in a fast-paced organization found themselves overwhelmed and reactive, believing this was just how work had to be. They lacked intentionality in their approach, resulting in stress, strained relationships and even burn-out. When they were introduced to the concept of 'working by design', it transformed their experience. They realized they had agency to create habits, time-block their schedules and redesign their meetings to suit their needs.

The shift to intentionality empowered them to see work as an opportunity to improve their effectiveness, which positively impacted both individual and team performance. This collective realization led to a shared plan to redesign their approach and stay accountable to their new practices.

Team culture as a product in development

Designing team culture is a creative process, much like developing a product. It involves identifying the

Design: designing ways of working

'bugs' or pain points that hinder performance and experimenting with solutions. Teams can use techniques such as design thinking, for example applying the Design Council's helpful 'Double Diamond' model of discovery, definition, development and delivery.[17]

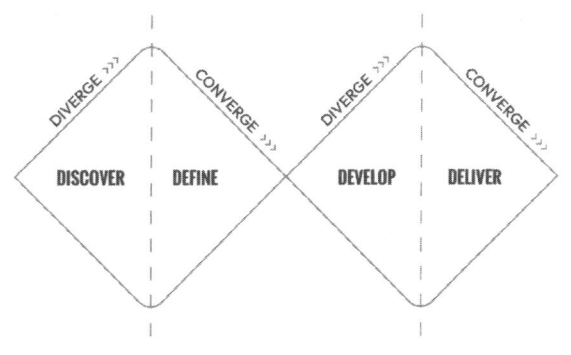

Figure 2 Design Council's 'Double Diamond'. Redrawn by Gabija Jankauskaite; reproduced with permission.

1. **Discover:** Identify pain points that prevent great work.
2. **Define:** Pinpoint the true problem to solve.
3. **Develop:** Brainstorm potential solutions.
4. **Deliver:** Test a solution as an experiment.

By approaching culture as a living system that evolves, teams can foster an open mindset and prioritize continuous improvement. This also creates psychological safety, as everyone knows they are experimenting together and learning as they go.

The power of routines and rituals

Routines and rituals are practical tools for embedding desired team behaviours into daily work.

- **Routines** are structured sequences of actions, like a regular meeting rhythm or a project retrospective.
- **Rituals** have deeper social meaning, marking moments of connection or purpose, such as celebrating milestones or starting meetings with a check-in.

Unlike one-off team-building activities, routines and rituals are integrated into everyday work, creating consistent opportunities for connection and collaboration. For example, a retrospective meeting might serve as both a routine for extracting learnings and a ritual for celebrating a project's completion.

Benefits of routines and rituals

- **Integration:** Turn desired behaviours into habits.

Design: designing ways of working

- **Reduction of cognitive load:** Free up mental capacity for creativity and problem-solving.
- **Creation of safety and familiarity:** Provide stability in times of uncertainty.

Teams can align their routines and rituals with their values, strengthening their identity and reinforcing collaboration.

Optimizing team productivity

1. Designing for team flow

Flow is a state of deep focus and engagement that leads to high performance.[18] For teams, 'group flow' happens when members are fully immersed in a shared activity, balancing individual contributions with collective goals.[19]

Facilitators often design workshops to achieve this kind of flow by setting clear goals, creating structure and allowing space for creative breakthroughs. Teams can adopt similar principles:

- Use shared goals and clarity to focus efforts.
- Foster open communication and active listening.
- Balance individual autonomy with collaboration.

2. Managing overwhelm and workload

A design approach can help teams manage workloads and prevent burn-out. One effective technique is a 'task braindump', where team members list all their responsibilities then organize them into themes. This creates a visual representation of the team's workload, revealing overlaps, redundancies or gaps in capacity.

With a clear view of responsibilities, the team can set priorities and define 'high performance' standards that balance ambition with realism. This process encourages transparency, shared accountability and a focus on meaningful work.

3. Transparency to support work

Transparency is essential for effective collaboration. It ensures team members have the information they need to do their work and fosters accountability. Tools like kanban boards or shared project management systems can help teams visualize tasks and track progress.

However, these tools are only effective when paired with a commitment to open communication. Teams should create clear processes for sharing updates, organizing files and deciding when to use different communication channels (e.g. email versus instant messaging).

Design: designing ways of working

Designing for connection

Collaboration is about balancing individual and collective work. Teams should intentionally design both the times they come together (meetings, workshops) and the spaces in between (asynchronous work).

Asynchronous work

Asynchronous work allows team members to contribute on their own schedule, providing flexibility and reducing the need for constant meetings. To make this approach successful:

- Clearly define expectations for contributions, deadlines and formats.
- Use collaboration tools to keep everyone aligned.
- Emphasize that asynchronous work is part of the overall team effort, not a secondary task.

Remote and hybrid teams

Remote and hybrid teams require additional intentionality to maintain connection and culture. Strategies include:

- scheduling regular in-person retreats for fully remote teams
- designing specific activities for in-office days in hybrid teams
- creating virtual co-working sessions for mutual accountability and focus

Technology as a tool for design

Digital tools have revolutionized teamwork, but they can also overwhelm if not used thoughtfully. Teams should design how they use technology to support their unique needs, from task management to file organization.

Questions to consider:

- When should we use instant messaging versus email?
- How do we organize shared files for easy access?
- What processes ensure our tools enhance, rather than hinder, productivity?

By proactively addressing these details, teams can prevent miscommunication and wasted time, ensuring their tools serve their goals.

Design: designing ways of working

The impact of intentional design

Designing how a team works isn't about imposing rigid rules – it's about creating flexible systems that evolve with the team's needs. By combining intentionality, creativity and collaboration, teams can overcome challenges, foster stronger connections and unlock their full potential.

With design as a pillar, teams move from reacting to their environment to shaping it – becoming empowered, resilient and high performing.

So what? Over to you…

1. Where have you noticed your team working 'by default' rather than 'by design'?

2. How could you use rituals and routines to better improve connection and performance?

Design: designing ways of working

3. How could you experiment with asynchronous tools and working to support progress?

Day 9
Change: continuous improvement

Change is the cornerstone of creating a high-performing team culture. Without it, all the strategies and principles discussed in this framework remain theoretical. True transformation happens when new ideas are implemented and sustained as part of the team's daily routines. This chapter focuses on how teams can adopt and embed behaviour changes to build a culture of continuous improvement.

Making tiny tweaks, not sweeping changes

Effective change doesn't require grand gestures. Small, incremental improvements can have significant impacts. For example:

- **Saying hello:** A company striving to embody its value of 'consideration' identified a simple action: greeting colleagues each morning. This tiny adjustment fostered a more caring culture and set a positive tone for employees' days.
- **Incorporating creative nudges:** To encourage everyday creativity, one team incorporated ideation techniques into their routine. Regular reminders via their chat platform kept these techniques top of mind until they became ingrained habits.
- **Reflecting for 15 minutes a week:** A team facing constant 'urgent and important' tasks redefined their identity by setting aside 15 minutes weekly for reflection and professional development, allowing them to focus on 'important but not urgent' work.

A new approach to change

Workshops are just the beginning

A workshop might spark new ideas, but the real work lies in sustaining momentum afterward. Teams must translate insights into action and adapt existing habits to ensure progress continues.

Facilitators understand that behaviour change requires commitment. Without deliberate follow-up, ideas generated in a workshop often fail to materialize into impactful change.

Understanding team habits

Habits shape how individuals and teams operate. These can be grouped into three categories:

1. **Individual habits:** how people personally organize their work and time
2. **Collaboration habits:** the way team members interact, such as giving feedback or sharing information
3. **Team habits:** the collective behaviours that define how a team functions, including meeting styles, communication norms and decision-making processes

To identify team habits, observe patterns in interactions, communication styles and decision-making dynamics. Encourage the team to reflect on these behaviours, highlighting those that support or hinder productivity and engagement.

Change: continuous improvement

Change as a continuous process

High-performing teams treat change as an ongoing process rather than a one-time initiative. They continuously evaluate and refine their habits, adapting to new challenges and opportunities.

The role of adaptability

Research by Chatman et al. highlights that successful teams have clear behavioural goals but remain flexible to external changes.[20] This adaptability ensures that teams stay effective in dynamic environments.

Overcoming barriers to change

Why change is hard

Change often fails because it requires overcoming deeply ingrained habits. Neuroscience shows that forming new habits involves creating entirely new neural pathways, which takes time and effort.

- **Effort versus ease:** Our brains favour familiar routines, even when they're unproductive.
- **Limited willpower:** Self-control diminishes as we expend mental energy throughout the

day, making it harder to adopt new behaviours under stress.

Strategies for change

1. **Make change easy:** Break large goals into small, actionable steps. For example, instead of aiming for 'better collaboration', start with simple actions like sharing one new idea during each team meeting.
2. **Leverage environmental cues:** Design your environment to encourage desired behaviours, such as by disabling distracting notifications or using visual reminders.
3. **Prioritize consistency:** Regular, small actions are more effective than sporadic grand gestures. Track progress to build momentum and encourage accountability.
4. **Use habit stacking:** Pair new behaviours with existing routines. For instance, add a reflective question at the end of meetings to encourage continuous learning.

Motivating your team to change

Ryan and Deci's self-determination theory[21] identifies three factors critical to sustaining motivation:

Change: continuous improvement

- **Competence:** Ensure tasks are appropriately challenging.
- **Autonomy:** Allow team members to approach tasks in their own way.
- **Relatedness:** Help the team understand the importance of their work and its connection to shared goals.

The **Alignment pillar** of the framework in this book ensures teams have a clear vision and purpose, laying the foundation for motivation and successful change.

Facilitating collective change

Collective implementation intentions

Implementation intention is a concept that takes goal setting one step further. It demonstrates that when we are specific about when, how and where we will perform a new action and we specify how we will counteract any barriers, a new action is more likely to stick.[22] This is described as an 'if-then' statement. Teams can use these statements to formalize responses to common challenges. For example: 'If we encounter competing priorities, then we will reassess based on our team values.'

This shared commitment ensures everyone is aligned and accountable when obstacles arise.

Continue-Stop-Start framework

This tool helps teams evaluate and refine their habits:

- **Continue:** Identify successful practices to maintain.
- **Stop:** Pinpoint unproductive behaviours to eliminate.
- **Start:** Introduce new habits to improve performance.

A useful tool to help you plot potential new ideas so that you can identify those that are easy to implement yet deliver significant results is the Impact Effort Matrix,[23] developed by Bjørn Andersen, Tom Fagerhaug and Marti Beltz; this will help you decide which actions to prioritize.

Embedding change into daily work

Change becomes sustainable when it's integrated into regular team routines. This can be done through:

1. **Micro-actions:** Encourage small, achievable commitments after each meeting or workshop.

Change: continuous improvement

2. **Reflection:** Regularly review progress to identify barriers and refine strategies.
3. **Nudges and reminders:** Use prompts (e.g., calendar notifications) to reinforce desired behaviours.
4. **Tracking progress visually:** Shared dashboards or trackers encourage accountability and celebrate success.

By embedding these practices into daily operations, teams can maintain momentum and foster a culture of continuous improvement.

So what? Over to you…

1. What team habits have you observed, and do they support collaboration?

2. What tools and strategies might you use to make collective change easier in your team?

Change: continuous improvement

3. How can you monitor and celebrate progress in your team?

Day 10
Great teams that last

You're ready to start building great teams! But how do you sustain this new approach in the months and years ahead?

Let's review the five pillars of high-performing teams:

1. **Alignment:** Define your team's purpose and values.
2. **Cohesion:** Build empathy and self-awareness to foster stronger connections.
3. **Communication:** Enhance interactions through facilitation skills.
4. **Design**: Create routines, rituals and systems that support productivity.
5. **Change:** Embed behaviour changes to sustain growth.

Underpinning these pillars are four foundations of a workshop culture:

1. Workshops are more than a one-off event.
2. Balance creativity and productivity.
3. Make tiny tweaks, not sweeping changes.
4. A workshop culture is intentionally designed.

Keep coming back to this framework, particularly when your team has experienced a change – a team member joins or leaves, the nature of work that you're doing changes (e.g. because of a new client or initiative) or something in your wider environment shifts.

A new capability

Team culture development is a new capability that many of us have to train ourselves for. There are a range of techniques we can use to keep it a priority:

- **Creating nudges and reminders:** When we have a compelling vision for our team, which we translate into our values and then into behaviours, these can be expressed as micro-actions, as we just covered. We can create nudges and reminders to keep these micro-actions top of mind to subtly shift us in the right direction. This can be as simple as creating an email – scheduled or manual – with a question prompt, or a calendar invite that pops up as a notification, or as a question on your chat platform.

- **Making activity visible:** For a team, having visibility of your collective goals, as well as tracking contributions, can be a powerful way to demonstrate accountability. You can create shared spaces – a virtual or physical whiteboard, dashboard or counter system – that shows how many times someone has performed a new habit. Combine this with the idea of streaks and we can encourage gentle competition between team members. Remember to celebrate team members' activity when they've stayed accountable.
- **Integrating regular conversations into work:** Make sure to reinforce these interventions with regular conversations about progress and what people are experiencing through the change in your team meetings. Your team will learn from experimenting with new ideas in the real world as they come up against challenges in their daily work.

- **Testing, iteration and continuous improvement:** These systems set the foundation to change the fabric of your team. Experimentation becomes part of your culture, which builds an open mindset, psychological safety and a bias for reflection. This will gradually filter into other aspects of your work as you create an upward spiral in your team for more agility, adaptability and resilience.

Developing transferable skills

The focus of a workshop culture is on how your team changes the way they work. However, a secondary outcome is the skills they develop as a result. These include:

- strategic thinking
- creative thinking, problem-solving and ideation
- goal setting
- reflection and self-awareness
- empathy
- feedback and difficult conversations
- facilitation and meeting design
- active listening

- communication
- productivity and time management
- planning and scheduling
- design thinking
- behaviour change

These are transferable skills that are valuable across any role, team and project. A workshop culture can transform someone's approach to work and help them to become a better collaborator, therefore improving their opportunities for career growth and development.

Supporting your team

When a team undergoes a transformation, however gradual, this will impact the individuals in the team. The process of change can be challenging, as you'll be surfacing unproductive habits and re-forming the way your team works. The conversations you have, reflection you do and feedback you offer may lead a team member to become more aware of their deep-rooted habits and approaches that may be preventing their own and the team's development.

Facilitated workshops will open this up more than a usual meeting, but as team members are focused on forward momentum, there is still a limit to what they can cover. Sometimes there is a need to slow down so that the emotions and feelings that are emerging can be processed while a culture is shifting.

Additional coaching conversations – both individual and team based – can help your team members to navigate and break through these blocks, delve into conflicts or tensions that might arise as they do this work, build self-awareness and consider how they are showing up in the team.

Creating a plan for team culture development

How will you stay committed to team culture development?

You might start with a dedicated plan or roadmap to keep you accountable and focused. Then, as your team becomes more familiar with discussing your culture, you will find opportunities to connect it to other areas of your work – your annual strategic plan, team training or individual development plans.

At the start of your team's journey to a workshop culture, these conversations will be new and unfamiliar. However, the long-term goal is to eventually embed this into your ways of working and practices so that it defines the team's identity. It's what will differentiate you and keep you growing together so that you're a great team for life.

So what? Over to you…

1. What could you do to build your team culture in the next week?

2. What could you do to build your team culture in the next month?

3. What could you do to build your team culture over the next two to three quarters? (Remember to make your goals small and achievable, and create check-in points to review your progress.)

Conclusion

We've explored how creating a workshop culture can solve some of the root causes of ineffective collaboration in our organizations – bad meetings, lack of engagement and lack of purpose – and help us create more creative and productive teams.

A workshop culture can happen at the level of your team, even if it isn't common practice across your entire organization. This means taking responsibility for the factors that you can control and influence, one of which is how you work together as a team. It enables your team to create amazing value together, which ripples out to impact those you interact with – both internal and external stakeholders – who will also benefit from your more effective ways of working, clear communication and empathy.

And it doesn't stop there. A workshop culture has further potential to positively impact our working lives and businesses. Here are some ideas to consider:

Attracting and retaining talent

One of the main reasons that people leave their jobs for self-employment is to have more freedom, flexibility and autonomy, despite the uncertainty this may bring. A workshop culture creates flexibility within a supportive structure so that people can have more control over how they work. It gives leaders the tools to create this environment, potentially creating much more attractive workplaces where people want to stay.

More diverse and inclusive workplaces

A workshop culture has a big emphasis on celebrating and valuing the unique contribution of each team member. Teams design their ways of working by balancing individual needs with the collective goal. This means we can consider different requirements – for example, for working parents and those managing health conditions – and also be conscious of the nuances that come with race, gender, age and other diverse characteristics. By bringing people's identities to the centre, we can create the culture from there, rather than forcing anyone to conform into a rigid structure that doesn't suit them. This starts to create a more welcoming and inclusive workplace for people from all walks of life.

Conclusion

Supporting good mental health and well-being

As more people start to suffer from burn-out caused by overwhelming workloads and toxic workplaces, we need a new approach to mental health and well-being.

We tend to see work as something that is 'energy depleting'. We work hard and then take time away to recharge, or even recover. What if we were to see the potential of work for being 'energy giving' instead? Something that fulfils and nourishes us. We still value time away from work to refresh ourselves, but it meets a different purpose.

With a workshop culture, we design balance into the way that a team works. This means looking at time spent working alone and time spent together, noticing where there may be intense periods of work and where there are opportunities for downtime. We start to address one of the core reasons for work-based well-being challenges – unsustainable ways of working. We do not need to restore our physical and mental health. Our workplaces are instead designed so that they don't drain us in the first place. Or, even more radically, they become an environment that gives us more energy.

New ways of organizing and leading

A workshop culture can start to influence how we structure and lead our organizations, through:

- breaking down silos by creating more networked structures that bring talent together to collaborate from across departments and teams
- creating more iterative and frequent feedback and performance review processes that emphasize collaboration over competition in their reward structures
- exploring alternative career progression routes for individuals based on their interests, strengths and the contribution they bring, rather than offering one single upwards route
- rethinking leadership styles to create a more inclusive and consistent experience for employees across an organization (even if that's just starting with how meetings are run!)
- looking at new ways of developing strategy in a responsive way that invite in more voices from across an organization so that resilience and adaptability are built in

When we build more capacity for collaboration, we can reap tremendous results, as individuals and as organizations.

Conclusion

Because so much of our work happens in teams, we must pay particular attention to how we work together. If we make work a place where we can thrive, it means we have more space and energy to have a positive impact on the people around us.

Our work is one of the biggest opportunities we have to come into contact with people different from ourselves and learn how to collaborate effectively. It can be a springboard that makes us more curious about the world. We can build more empathy, appreciate diversity and learn how to have better conversations and resolve conflict. Then those skills become available for us to use in any situation, including in our personal relationships and our communities and in helping us towards a better society.

And it all starts with building better teams!

Endnotes

[1] B. Tabrizi, '75% of cross-functional teams are dysfunctional' in *Harvard Business Review* (23 June 2015). Available from https://hbr.org/2015/06/75-of-cross-functional-teams-are-dysfunctional (accessed 6 December 2024).

[2] Deloitte, 'Organizational performance: It's a team sport (2019 Global Human Capital Trends)' in *Deloitte Insights* (11 April 2019). Available from www2.deloitte.com/us/en/insights/focus/human-capital-trends/2019/team-based-organization.html (accessed 6 December 2024).

[3] Doodle, *The Doodle State of Meetings Report 2019* (2019). Available from https://assets.ctfassets.net/p24lh3qexxeo/axrPjsBSD1bLp2HYEqoij/d2f08c2aaf5a6ed80ee53b5ad7631494/Meeting_Report_2019.pdf (accessed 6 December 2024).

[4] S. Kauffeld and N. Lehmann-Willenbrock, 'Meetings matter: Effects of work group communication on organizational success' in *Small Group Research*, 43 (April), 130–158 (2012).

[5] J. A. Allen and S. G. Rogelberg, 'Manager-led group meetings: A context for promoting employee engagement' *in Group & Organization Management: An International Journal*, 38 (5), 543–569 (2013).

[6] J. Harter, 'Dismal employee engagement is a sign of global mismanagement' in *Gallup* (20 December 2017). Available from https://news.gallup.com/opinion/gallup/224012/dismal-employee-engagement-sign-global-mismanagement.aspx (accessed 6 December 2024).

Endnotes

[7] J. K. Harter, F. L. Schmidt, and T. L. Hayes, 'Business-unit-level relationship between employee satisfaction, employee engagement, and business outcomes: A meta-analysis' in *Journal of Applied Psychology*, 87 (2), 268–279 (2002).

[8] T. Amabile and S. Kramer, *The Progress Principle: Using small wins to ignite joy, engagement and creativity at work* (2011).

[9] S. Achor, A. Reece, G. Rosen Kellerman and Á. Robichaux, '9 out of 10 people are willing to earn less money to do more meaningful work' in *Harvard Business Review* (6 November 2018). Available from https://hbr.org/2018/11/9-out-of-10-people-are-willing-to-earn-less-money-to-do-more-meaningful-work (accessed 10 June 2023).

[10] C. Duhigg, 'What Google learned from its quest to build the perfect team' in *The New York Times Magazine* (25 February 2016). Available from https://www.nytimes.com/2016/02/28/magazine/what-google-learned-from-its-quest-to-build-the-perfect-team.html (accessed 6 December 2024).

[11] A. 'Sandy' Pentland, 'The new science of building great teams' in *Harvard Business Review* (April 2012). Available from https://hbr.org/2012/04/the-new-science-of-building-great-teams (accessed 6 December 2024).

[12] S. Covey, *The 7 Habits of Highly Effective People* (2013).

[13] C. S. Dweck, *Mindset: How you can fulfil your potential* (2012).

[14] D. Pink, *Drive: The surprising truth about what motivates us* (2011).

[15] HBS Communications, 'Problem-solving techniques take on new twist' in *The Harvard Gazette* (15 August 2018). Available from https://news.harvard.edu/gazette/story/2018/08/collaborate-on-complex-problems-but-only-intermittently/ (accessed 16 December 2024).

[16] D. Gray, 'Empathy map' in *Gamestorming* (14 July 2017). Available from https://gamestorming.com/empathy-mapping/ (accessed 6 December 2024).

[17] Design Council, *History of the Double Diamond*. Available from www.designcouncil.org.uk/our-resources/the-double-diamond/history-of-the-double-diamond/ (accessed 6 December 2024).

[18] M. Csikszentmihalyi, *Flow: The psychology of optimal experience* (1990). Csikszentmihalyi published several books on 'flow'. This is just one!

[19] K. Sawyer, 'Group flow and group genius' in *The NAMTA Journal*, 40 (3), 29–52 (Summer 2015).

[20] J. A. Chatman, D. F. Caldwell, C. A. O'Reilly and B. Doerr, 'Parsing organizational culture: How the norm for adaptability influences the relationship between culture consensus and financial performance in high-technology firms' in *Journal of Organizational Behavior*, 35 (6), 785–808 (2014).

[21] R. M. Ryan and E. L. Deci, 'Self-determination theory and the facilitation of intrinsic motivation, social development, and well-being' in *American Psychologist*, 55 (1), 68–78 (2000).

[22] P. M. Gollwitzer, 'Implementation intentions' in *American Psychologist*, 54 (7), 493–503 (1999).

[23] ASQ, *Impact Effort Matrix*. Available from https://asq.org/quality-resources/impact-effort-matrix (accessed 6 December 2024).

Enjoyed this? Then you'll love…

Workshop Culture: A guide to building teams that thrive by Alison Coward

What if every day at work felt like your team's most productive 'away day'?

The most successful and innovative teams and organizations are highly collaborative, creative and productive – you will find the principles of great workshops infused throughout their culture.

This is a book about how running great workshops, and taking inspiration from them, can lead to a great team environment. *Workshop Culture* will show you how to create a happy and engaged team through small actions that lead to big results. It features a practical and accessible toolkit to help improve your team's performance and productivity.

Workshop Culture gives you:

- inspiring case studies from forward-thinking and innovative teams that have found success from a workshop culture

- a structured methodology that you can follow to bring more happiness, productivity and engagement to your team
- practical exercises to help you build new skills and knowledge, and increase impact at work

Alison Coward is a team culture coach, consultant and founder of Bracket, a consultancy that partners with ambitious, forward-thinking companies to build high-performing, collaborative team cultures.

Other 6-Minute Smarts titles

Do Change Better (based on *How to be a Change Superhero* by Lucinda Carney)

How to be Happy at Work (based on *My Job Isn't Working!* by Michael Brown)

How to Get to Know Your Customer (based on *Do Penguins Eat Peaches?* by Katie Tucker)

The Listening Leader (based on *The Listening Shift* by Janie Van Hool)

Mastering People Management (based on *Mission: To Manage* by Marianne Page)

No-Nonsense PR (based on *Hype Yourself* by Lucy Werner)

Present Like a Pro (based on *Executive Presentations* by Jacqui Harper)

Reimagine Your Career (based on *Work/Life Flywheel* by Ollie Henderson)

Sales Made Simple (based on *More Sales Please* by Sara Nasser Dalrymple)

The Speed Storytelling Toolkit (based on *Exposure* by Felicity Cowie)

Write to Think (based on *Exploratory Writing* by Alison Jones)

Look out for more titles coming soon! Visit www.practicalinspiration.com for all our latest titles.